I0698291

Bee fact #1

Bees have 5 eyes.

Bee fact #2

Bees can't see the color red.

Bee fact #3

Bees help plants grow.

Bee fact #4

Honeybees can only sting one time.

Busy Bees Facts

Bee fact #5

Many bees live together in hives.

Bee fact #6

Bee wings make a loud buzzing sound.

Bee fact #7

A beekeeper takes care of bees.

Bee fact #8

Some bees live alone.

Busy Bees Facts

Bee fact #9

There are over 20,000 species of bees.

Bee fact #10

A honey bee can fly up
to 15 miles per hour.

Bee fact #11

A bee makes a teaspoon of honey in its lifetime.

Bee fact #12

A beehive can hold about 50,000 bees.

Bee fact #13

Bees have 6 legs.

Bee fact #14

The queen lays 20,000 eggs per day.

Bee fact #15

Bees like the sweet
smell of flowers.

Bee fact #16

The colors that attract bees most are purple, violet, and blue.

Bee fact #17

Bees like to drink nectar.

Bee fact #18

In the winter, bees form a cluster in the hive to stay warm.

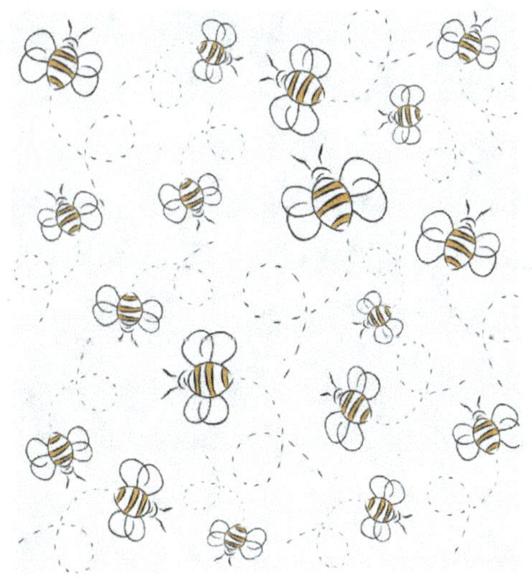

Busy Bees Facts

Bee fact #19

The food bees like most is called pollen.

Bee fact #20

Bees help produce the food
we eat.

BEES ARE SO IMPORTANT TO US!

Do you know any more fun facts? Use the doodle pages to jot them down.

Busy Bees Doodle Page

Busy Bees Doodle Page

Busy Bees Doodle Page

Busy Bees Doodle Page

Busy Bees Doodle Page

Busy Bees Facts

Busy Bees Doodle Page

Busy Bees Doodle Page

Busy Bees Doodle Page

Busy Bees Doodle Page

Busy Bees Doodle Page

Busy Bees Facts

Busy Bees Doodle Page

Busy Bees Doodle Page

Busy Bees Doodle Page

Busy Bees Doodle Page

Busy Bees Doodle Page

Busy Bees Doodle Page

Busy Bees Doodle Page

Busy Bees Doodle Page

That was fun! Now, check out our
Busy Bees Writing Practice book
&
Busy Bees Gratitude Journal
On Amazon.

www.ingramcontent.com/pod-product-compliance
Lightning Source LLC
Chambersburg PA
CBHW051912250726

48659CB00002B/608